Mornings
Like This

MORNINGS LIKE THIS

FOUND POEMS

ANNIE DILLARD

HarperCollins*Publishers*

Some of the poems in this book have appeared in *Antaeus, The Atlantic, Common Knowledge, Double Take, Field, The Georgia Review, Harper's, Harvard Review, The Kenyon Review, The Nantucket Review, New Letters, The New Republic, Ontario Review, Parnassus, Poetry,* and *Southwest Review.*

HarperCollins books may be purchased for educational, business, or sales promotional use. For information, please write: Special Markets Department, HarperCollins Publishers, Inc., 10 East 53rd Street, New York, NY 10022.

FIRST EDITION

Designed by Gloria Adelson/LuLu Graphics.

ISBN 0-06-017155-3

95 96 97 98 99 CC/HC 10 9 8 7 6 5 4 3 2 1

for Carin

CONTENTS

Author's Note

Poetry books seldom require explanation, but this one does. Excepting only some titles and subtitles, I did not write a word of it. Other hands composed the poems' lines—the poems' sentences. These are found poems. They differ substantially, however, from what we usually think of as found poems.

Usually those happy poets (including me) who write found poetry go pawing through popular culture like sculptors on trash heaps. They hold and wave aloft usable artifacts and fragments: jingles and ad copy, menus and broadcasts—all objets trouvés, the literary equivalents of Warhol's Campbell's soup cans and Duchamp's bicycle. By entering a found text as a poem, the poet doubles its context. The original meaning remains intact, but now it swings between two poles. The poet adds, or at any rate increases, the element of delight. This is an urban, youthful, ironic, cruising kind of poetry. It serves up whole texts, or uninterrupted fragments of texts.

This volume, instead of presenting whole texts as "found," offers poems built from bits of broken text. The poems are original as poems; their themes and their orderings are invented. Their sentences are not. Their sentences come from the books named. I lifted them. Sometimes I dropped extra words; I never added a word.

Some of the section headings are my own ("A Comical Question for Boys"). Most come from the books themselves, even the wondrous heading from *Junior High School English,* "Studying and Making Little Poems Packed with Meaning."

In the course of composing such found poems, the original authors' intentions were usually first to go. A nineteenth-century Russian memoir of hunting and natural history yields a poem about love and death. A book of nineteenth-century oceanographic data yields a poem about seeing. A nineteenth-century manual of boys' projects yields a poem about growing old—and so forth. Others, of course, pin down less readily.

Two of these poems raise other points.

The New Testament Apocrypha is a loose collection of written legends and, chiefly, torn and damaged fragments. Scholar-editors print such texts carefully to show—using ellipses and question marks—where fragments break off and which translations are guesses. An edition of the New Testament Apocrypha yields a poem about the baffling quality of Christ's utterances and the absurdly fragmentary nature of spiritual knowledge. Like many of these poems, it looks surprisingly sober on the page.

It certainly does not do to rob a brilliant literary stylist of sentences, rearrange them as poetry, and fob off the work as one's own. Consequently the poem "Mayakovsky in New York" requires explanation, for Mayakovsky was a poet quite before I took wild liberties. He wrote his own poems about United States cities (ably edited by Patricia Blake in *The Bedbug and Selected Poetry*). The prose text I mined here, however, is a hastily written piece of travel journalism of some sixty-one pages. Its subject meets only glancingly the poem's subject.

This is editing at its extreme: writing without composing. Half the poems seek to serve poetry's oldest and most sincere aims with one of its newest and most ironic methods, to dig deep with a shallow tool. The other half are just jokes.

We are not interested in tree limbs
Weighted with Spanish moss.
What we want to know is
Why arms go limp.

Is it the pain of blocking
Too many hooks? Is it the aching
That comes from throwing
Too many punches too soon?

We want facts, not French phrases.

—A letter to *Sports Illustrated*
by James P. Lewandowski, Toledo, Ohio. February 18, 1974

I want to use the world rather than my own invention.

—Ellsworth Kelly, *The Painter's Eye*

Mornings
Like This

Dash It

—Mikhail Prishvin, *Nature's Diary*, 1925, translated
by L. Navrozov

How wonderfully it was all arranged that each
Of us had not too long to live. This is one
Of the main snags—the shortness of the day.
The whole wood was whispering, "Dash it, dash it . . ."

What joy—to walk along that path! The snow
Was so fragrant in the sun! What a fish!
Whenever I think of death, the same stupid
Question arises: "What's to be done?"

As for myself, I can only speak of what
Made me marvel when I saw it for the first time.
I remember my own youth when I was in love.
I remember a puddle rippling, the insects aroused.

I remember our own springtime when my lady told me:
You have taken my best. And then I remember
How many evenings I have waited, how much
I have been through for this one evening on earth.

Mornings Like This

—David Grayson, *The Countryman's Year*, 1936

Sunday. What still sunny days
We have now. And I alone in them.
So brief—our best!

So much is wrong, but not my hills.
I have been thinking of writing
A letter to the President of China.

Do it, do it, do it, do it.
I beseech you, I beseech you,
I beseech you, I beseech you.

Mornings like this: I look
About the earth and the heavens:
There is not *enough* to believe—

Mornings like this. How heady
The morning air! How sharp
And sweet and clear the morning air!

Authentic winter! The odor of campfires!
Beans eighteen inches long!
A billion chances—and I am here!

And here I lie in the quiet room
And read and read and read.
So easy—so easy—so easy.

Pools in old woods, full of leaves.
Give me time enough in this place
And I will surely make a beautiful thing.

The Handy Boy

—D. C. Beard, *The American Boys Handy Book*,
1882

INDEX

Every Boy His Own Ice-Boat;
Every Boy His Own Bubble Pipe;
Every boy a decorative artist.

How to Make a Blowgun.
How to Bind a Prisoner Without a Cord.
How to Rig and Sail Small Boats.
Practical Taxidermy for Boys:
       Let us suppose an owl
       Has been lowering around, and that you
       Have shot the rascal. Do not
       Throw him away. What a splendid
       Ornament he will make for the library!
       He must be skinned and stuffed!

QUESTIONS

What boy can sit all day in a boat
Without experiencing a longing
For some new patent transparent diving bell?

Who can watch machinery of any kind in motion, without
Experiencing an indefinable sort of pleasure?

SNOW STATUARY

It is very seldom that pigs
Are sculptured in marble or cast
In bronze, and it would be well
To make some of snow, so as to have
Statues not likely to be found elsewhere.

A statue of a Frenchman in an ulster
Is also rather uncommon.

FILLING THE GAPS IN LONG WINTER EVENINGS

There will frequently occur gaps,
In the long winter evenings, that are hard
To fill up satisfactorily . . .

HOW TO MAKE THE DANCING FAIRIES, THE BATHER, AND THE ORATOR

How to Make a Handkerchief Doll:
As the music becomes lively the handkerchiefs
Lose their diffidence and dance about
In a very active manner.

The Bather: If among the company
There be any who are familiar
With the scenes at seaside summer resorts,
They will be convulsed with laughter.

The Orator: When the fingers are moved
Around in mimic gestures,
The effect is comical beyond measure.
The little man can be made
To scratch his nose, roll up sleeves . . .

Many other effects I used
To produce in my puppet-shows
At present escape my memory.

PERSONAL NOTES

Upon opening his eyes one late
Summer morning the author
Was very much startled and astonished
At an apparition he beheld on the wall.

As the writer was passing along Broadway
The other day, he saw an old acquaintance.

Many rare fish have I eaten in my time.

Long and loud were the shouts
Of laughter of my companions.

OMINOUS PERSONAL NOTES

With paper fireworks an enjoyable
Day may be spent and the glorious
Fourth of July passed with no danger
Of such a painful accident as happened
To the writer July 4, 1884,
But from which he fully recovered.

ENVOY

It is not without regret
That the author bids farewell.
It is hard to lay down the pen
And again plunge into the busy world
Along with other old boys the tops
Of whose heads begin to resemble
What the lads in Kentucky called "alleys,"
A sort of flesh-colored marble or "Meg"
With faint blue veins on it,
Very hard and very shiny.

The Pathfinder of the Seas

—Matthew Fontaine Maury, *Maritime Conference
Held at Brussels, Devising a Uniform System of
Meteorological Observations at Sea;* August and
September, 1853; and *Explanations and Sailing
Directions to Accompany the Wind and Current
Charts,* 1858

The sea is very wide. The tooth of running
Water is very sharp. And why have not
The currents of the sea worn away its bottom?

Note the direction of the winds which bring the rain.
Note anything that is particular about rainbows.
Draw up a bucket of water anywhere.

With regard to hail, describe the stones,
And any peculiarity connected with the snow-flakes.
Enter also sea-weed, driftwood . . . shooting-stars . . .

Tide-rips at sea . . . showers of dust
And red fogs . . . Aurora Borealis . . .
Waterspouts . . . the height and velocity of waves.

If the water which now lies on the floor
Of the deep sea has to lie there forever,
Why was it made fluid instead of solid?

Mention the time when the dew commences to fall.
Do not the clouds, night and day, now
Present themselves to us in a new light?

The Sign of Your Father

—E. Hennecke, *New Testament Apocrypha*, Vol. I,
edited by Wilhelm Schneemelcher, English
translation edited by R. McL. Wilson, 1963

I

(The grain of wheat) . . .
Place shut in . . .
It was laid beneath and invisible . . .
Its wealth imponderable?

And as they were in perplexity
At his strange question, Jesus
On his way came (to the) bank
Of the (riv)er Jordan,
Stretched out (hi)s right
Hand, (fill)ed it with . . .
And sowed . . . on the . . .
And then . . . water . . . And . . .
Before (their eyes),
Brought fruit . . . much
To the jo(y?) . . .

Jesus said: "Become
Passers-by."

He said: "Lord, there are many
Around the cistern, but
Nobody in the cistern."

And we said to him, "O Lord,
Are you speaking again

In parables to us?" And he said
To us, "Do not be grieved . . ."

II

(His) disciples ask him (and s)ay:
How should we fas(t and how
Should we pr)ay and how (. . .
. . .) and what should we observe
(Of the traditions?) Jesus says (. . . . .
. . . . .) do not (. . . . .
. . . . .) truth (. . . . .
. . . . .) hidden (. . . . .

"This saying has been handed down
In a particularly sorry condition."

They all wondered and were afraid.
The Redeemer (σωτήρ) smiled
And spake to them: Of what
Are you thinking, or (ή) about what
Are you at a loss (ἀπορεῖν), or
(ή) what are you seeking?

If they ask you: "What
Is the sign of your Father in you?"
You say to them: "It is a movement
And a rest (ἀνάπαυσις)."

An Acquaintance in the Heavens

—Martha Evans Martin, who seemed lonely in *The Friendly Stars*, 1907, revised by Donald Howard Menzel, 1964

A window in my bedroom opens towards
The northeast. Many times I have suddenly
Opened my eyes in the night. Betelgeuse
Pushes its red face up over the horizon.

> One begins in February to watch the handle
> Of the Dipper, so clearly pointing to something
> Important just below the horizon.

> It has pulled into the view the steady
> Shining face of Arcturus. The hawks
> And crows are among the high trees.

There comes a soft June evening. The blue
Jays have become stealthy. One walks
To the end of the porch and looks for Altair.

> Orion: We watch for it in October.
> One jewel after another emerges
> From the storehouse below the horizon until

> The whole splendid figure is before us.
> We remember then that the juncos
> Came that day and we heard them.

The birds have ceased to sing and are seeking
Shadows. Fomalhaut the lonely:
When the days are growing shorter, some evening,

Just after dark, one sees it, trailing
Over the small arc of its circle
With no companion near it, and no need.

I Am Trying to Get at Something Utterly Heartbroken

—V. van Gogh, letters, 1873–1890, edited by
I. Stone, translated by Johanna van Gogh

I

At the end of the road is a small cottage,
And over it all the blue sky.
I am trying to get at something utterly heartbroken.

The flying birds, the smoking chimneys,
And that figure loitering below in the yard—
If we do not learn from this, then from what shall we learn?

The miners go home in the white snow at twilight.
These people are quite black. Their houses are small.
The time for making dark studies is short.

A patch of brown heath through which a white
Path leads, and sky just delicately tinged,
Yet somewhat passionately brushed.
We who try our best to live, why do we not live more?

II

The branches of poplars and willows rigid like wire.
It may be true that there is no God here,
But there must be one not far off.

A studio with a cradle, a baby's high chair.
Those colors which have no name
Are the real foundation of everything.

What I want is more beautiful huts far away on the heath.
If we are tired, isn't it then because
We have already walked a long way?

The cart with the white horse brings
A wounded man home from the mines.
Bistre and bitumen, well applied,
Make the colouring ripe and mellow and generous.

III

A ploughed field with clods of violet earth;
Over all a yellow sky with a yellow sun.
So there is every moment something that moves one intensely.

A bluish-grey line of trees with a few roofs.
I simply could not restrain myself or keep
My hands off it or allow myself to rest.

A mother with her child, in the shadow
Of a large tree against the dune.
To say how many green-greys there are is impossible.

I love so much, so very much, the effect
Of yellow leaves against green trunks.
This is not a thing that I have sought,
But it has come across my path and I have seized it.

The Hunter

—Mikhail Prishvin, *Nature's Diary*, 1925, translated
by L. Navrozov

Do you know how a hunter's heart unfolds?
I walked over the snow—the crust held.
I stopped to listen. The fox came towards me.

It takes no more than ten minutes to describe the features
Of the day. It's only a split second a man
Needs to remove his safety-catch. Yet when I glanced
At the safety-catch and removed it, it was too late.

I kept inshore. I thought I heard a nightingale.
A blue animal path running across the vast field.
A full moon, a Venus as large as my fist,
The Great Bear and the entire vaultful of stars.

What I saw over the sight was quite different from what
Could be seen with the ordinary eye. My head was clear.

One lacks words to describe what the deep forest
Is like at night when you know that the great birds
Are asleep overhead. I lack words to give
Even a pale description of all this marshland.

In the mist the artist stole up very close and took aim.
It was like aiming at the rising moon. The mind
Works in infinite spaces—yet haphazardly, spreading.

Observations and Experiments

—Alan Dale, *Observations and Experiments in Natural History,* 1960

OBSERVATIONS

Observations are usually
Not too difficult to make.

1.

When I was living in Tamworth,
One year, towards the end of September,
Many of the leaves of my cherry tree
Became rather odd in appearance.

2.

Trout seem to learn that danger
Is associated with artificial flies;
Perhaps it is the hook in them.

3.

I once saw a frog attacked
And turned over by my dog
And it lay quite still on its back.

I am positive it made quite
A separate movement to put

Its front feet over its ears.
Why did it?

PERSONAL NOTE

There is a poem by John Drinkwater
Called *Pike Pool* which has always
Appealed strongly to me.

EXPERIMENTS

1.

Catch butterflies and clip
Their wings with scissors.
Do your observations
Outside, where butterflies are numerous.

2.

Pinch through ten worms.
Obtain a fresh herring and place it
On an open plate. Leave it.

3.

Liberate a grasshopper and cause
It to jump by touching it. Make
It jump again—and again.

Do its leaps get more feeble?
Does the insect become more reluctant
To jump again after each leap?

LAST PERSONAL NOTE

Once I was walking across fields in Shropshire
To a river which, because of a rise
In the ground, I could not see.

I have preferred to know
Less and less about more and more.

The Child in Spring

—Max Picard, *The World of Silence*, 1948,
translated by Stanley Godman, 1952

Suddenly, the green appears on the trees—as if
The green passed silently from one tree to another.
Children suddenly appear out of the chinks.
They throw their balls high up in the air.

The child is like a little hill of silence.
Children—little hills of silence—are scattered
Everywhere in the world of words. Birds

Throw notes of their song like balls against
The silence, as in a game. The word is led
By silence to the edge of the child's mouth.

It is as though each syllable had to detach
Separately from the silence. The child gazes
After its word as it might watch its ball in the air.

Class Notes on Painting and the Arts

—Robert Henri, *The Art Spirit* (compiled by his
student, Margery A. Ryerson), 1923

TO BEGIN

Get a right height of chair
And sit at your painting table.

THE EYEBROWS

The eyebrows are important. They have great meaning.
They are never without important action.

Be certain of them, their place, direction,
Length, beginning, variation, and end.

The eyebrows are hair in the last instance.
What use will you make of the eyebrow?

HAIR

Ask yourself, what is your concept
Of the hair. How get its activity?

Let the hair flow amply over the head.
It goes back into richness.

The skull should be firm under the hair.
In hair there should be places of silence.

Look for the occurrence of beautiful measures in the hair.
Things are beautiful because they are related.

COLOR

There are many colors and they are all moving,
Moving. Color should flow over the face.

Brilliancy is going toward color, not white.
Color and warmth are coming into our lives.

LAUGHTER

The laughter should pass
From the beginning of the hair to the end of it.

A ripple runs around and picks up the chin.
When he laughs new forms begin.

After laughter one should feel full,
Not empty as one feels after fireworks.

THE HEAD

See the clock! Its great, big, blond
Full face is not spoiled

By the hands, as the face
Of your painting is by the features.

THE BODY

In nature it is the delicate yet strong turn
Of the *whole* neck which interests us.

Sometimes, however, the sterno-clido
Becomes the dominant interest.

The body is a solid.
Like the arm but larger.

FINAL EXHORTATIONS

Nothing should be negative, or trying to get away,
Brush strokes irresolute, words you did not mean.

You can do anything you want to do. What is rare
Is this actual wanting to do a specific thing.

QUESTION

What were the signs in that landscape,
In the air, in the motion, in our companionship,

That so excited our imagination
And made us so happy?

Mayakovsky in New York

—Vladimir Mayakovsky, *My Discovery of America*,
1926, in *America Through Russian Eyes*, edited
and translated by Olga Peters Hasty and Susanne Fusso

New York: You take a train that rips through versts.
It feels as if the trains were running over your ears.

For many hours the train flies along the banks
Of the Hudson about two feet from the water. At the stops,
Passengers run out, buy up bunches of celery,
And run back in, chewing the stalks as they go.

Bridges leap over the train with increasing frequency.

At each stop an additional story grows
Onto the roofs. Finally houses with squares
And dots of windows rise up. No matter how far
You throw back your head, there are no tops.

Time and again, the telegraph poles are made
Of wood. Maybe it only seems that way.

In the narrow canyons between the buildings, a sort
Of adventurer-wind howls and runs away
Along the versts of the ten avenues. Below
Flows a solid human mass. Only their yellow
Waterproof slickers hiss like samovars and blaze.

The construction rises and with it the crane, as if
The building were being lifted up off the ground
By its pigtail. It is hard to take it seriously.

The buildings are glowing with electricity; their evenly
Cut-out windows are like a stencil. Under awnings
The papers lie in heaps, delivered by trucks.
It is impossible to tear oneself away from this spectacle.

At midnight those leaving the theatres drink a last soda.
Puddles of rain stand cooling. Poor people scavenge
Bones. In all directions is a labyrinth of trains
Suffocated by vaults. There is no hope, your eyes
Are not accustomed to seeing such things.

They are starting to evolve an American gait out
Of the cautious steps of the Indians on the paths of empty
Manhattan. Maybe it only seems that way.

Light in the Open Air

—M. G. J. Minnaert, *The Nature of Light and Colour in the Open Air*, 1893, translated by H. M. Kremer-Priest

I

Everything described in this book is within
Your own powers of understanding and observation.

The Dark Inner Part,
The Bright Outer Part,
The Variability of the Colour of the Blue Sky.

> Try to imagine that you are looking at a painting
> And admire the evenness and delicacy of the transitions.

The Blue Sky:

> What is the explanation of this curious phenomenon?
> What can be the cause of this wonderful blue?

> Compare the blue of the sky with the skies
> Of Italy during your holiday.

The Colours of the Sun, Moon and Stars:

> It is difficult to judge the colour of the sun,
> Owing to its dazzling brightness. Personally,
> However, I should say it is decidedly yellow.

Be very cautious during these observations!
Do not overstrain your eyes!

Study the illumination . . .
Compare the light . . .
Compare the illumination . . .
Compare the luminosity . . .
Compare the light inside and outside a wood.

Intercept one of these images by a piece of paper.

II

Above all study your surroundings intently.

Move your opera glasses gently a little to the left,
Then to the right, and back again to the left . . .

> The colour of lakes,
> The colour of puddles along the road,
> Strong wind rising, grey sky.

> One more reason to keep our eyes open.

Which are the feeblest stars
Perceptible by you?

Practice on cold evenings.
Try to fill this gap. Notice
How much better you succeed with a little practice!

Estimate the strength of the ash-grey light
On a scale from 1 to 10.

Watch the separate breakers along the shore.

Imagine a pool of water in a hollow of the dunes . . .

Be sure to carry out this experiment!
It is as convincing as it is surprising!

Examine systematically the colours of the shadows!

Draw up a scale for the phosphorescence of the sea!

Everything is meant to be seen by you and done by you!

Always try to find the explanation.

This causes a very peculiar sensation,
Difficult to describe.

Stars

—Martha Evans Martin, *The Friendly Stars*, 1907,
revised by Donald Howard Menzel, 1964

To enjoy the constellations one must
Be satisfied not to expect too much of them.

Take them as we do our human friends:
Dragons fixed on the walls of the sky.

They hang during black nights under the dome.
Castor and Pollux: Two lusty-looking

Youths stand with their heads consolidated
Each wearing a star in his eye.

Cepheus: He stands with one foot on Polaris
And his head reaching to Andromeda. This comes

About because of confused mythology.
It has been discovered that Capella is not alone:

Another of nature's secret doors burst open
By pressure of zealous, untiring workers.

Occasionally one of the fainter stars
Calls for particular attention, as in the case

Of Mira, the Wonderful, in the Whale.
Pegasus: Ever on his back, he goes pawing

Across the heavens and down. The brevity of life,
However, does not stay the inquiring mind.

Junior High School English

—Briggs, McKinney, and Skeffington, *Junior High School English, For the Eighth Grade*, 1926

A CHALLENGE TO YOUR SPIRIT

Girls and boys of America, you
Are the hope of the world!
You can't evade it, young America.

And are you going to go on dancing
And spinning on your ear?
What are you thinking about, sitting

There staring into the dark?
Haven't you been lying around long
Enough? Shouldn't you go to work?

Find as interesting a subject as possible.
Write as vivid a sketch as you can
Of a person who attracts you or an animal.

SUGGESTIONS FOR SUBJECTS

How I Thought Out a Hard Sentence.
When My Chum and I Played Ghost.
        —A good one, don't you think?

A Lively Street Scene.
        —Except for a few, the people of Saint Louis
        Are not old timers, but are stylish and reformed.

28

Helping Father with the Threshing.
A letter from Telemachus to his mother.
　　　—"By crickets, there are big things in this world!"

Preparing Hog and Beef for Market.
Anchored in a Fog.
The Scum on Our Pond.

Think over what you have accomplished.
Was it all that you wished?
Has this story been told before?

The thought of the theme is good, but the form
Is poor. A sign of inexcusable
Carelessness or deplorable stupidity.

You should have learned by now to tell
A short story with a single point.
Why are the sentences so uninteresting?

Gott im Himmel! Practice. Improve
The wording. You have told enough
Untruths for one day. That will do.

STUDYING AND MAKING LITTLE POEMS PACKED
WITH MEANING

Here are some little poems and verses,
Each of which suggests a good deal
More than it tells. The details are signs:

　　　1. Gulls are strong of wing. Gulls
　　　　　Follow ships to sea. The sea
　　　　　Is deep. The moon is a cold body.

2. Nothing ever happens in this
   Slow town. The roads have been muddy
   For days. The red ants hasten.

3. When I was playin' wid my brudder,
   Happy was I. All round de little
   Farm I wandered when I was young.

Perhaps some of you would like to try
Putting into rhythmic form, in a few words
Full of meaning, some little scene you have felt.

Signals at Sea

—Charles H. Cugle, *Cugle's Practical Navigation,*
1936

*(If the flags in A's hoist cannot be made out, B keeps her
answering pennant at the "Dip" and hoists the signal "OWL"
or "WCX.")*

CXL	Do not abandon me.
A	I am undergoing a speed trial.
D	Keep clear of me—I am maneuvering with difficulty.
F	I am disabled. Communicate with me.
G	I require a pilot.
P	Your lights are out, or burning badly.
U	You are standing into danger.
X	Stop carrying out your intentions.
K	You should stop your vessel instantly.
L	You should stop. I have something important to communicate.
R	You may feel your way past me.

Emergencies

—Brent Q. Hafen, Ph.D., and Keith J. Karren, Ph.D.,
*Prehospital Emergency Care and Crisis
Intervention,* 1989

*(Few people are initially prepared for the sights, smells, and
sounds of intense human suffering.)*

FIRST THINGS FIRST

Introduce yourself to the patient.
If you have time and are in doubt,
Simply ask, "What
Would you like me to call you?"

Cut clothing away quickly
To see a bleeding site clearly.
Put on a pair of latex
Or surgical gloves to protect yourself . . .

Many religious people
Attach great significance
To religious symbols.
Unless it is necessary for treatment,
Do not remove crosses or amulets.

Observe circumstances, collect
Suicide notes, and compile
The relevant materials. Is the patient
Restless, irritable, or combative?

BYSTANDERS

It is best to wait rather
Than try to remove weapons
Or potential weapons from unstable
Victims, relatives, bystanders.

Ask someone, "Will you please
Turn off the TV?" Or do it yourself.

Say, "Please sit
On the ground on her left side,
Ma'am, and hold her hand.
Talk to her. Don't move
Her arm, and don't let her move
Her head. I'm going
To be checking her hips and legs."

Comment positively on the aid
Already given (for example,
"You've done a good job
Of immobilizing the head").

TOUCH

Take a hand, pat
A shoulder. Remember that
You have to be comfortable doing it,
And not just trying it as a gimmick.

Squeezing a foot or patting
An ankle, if you are working
Near the foot is not
Usually considered intimate.
Patting above the knee is.

Sometimes a man receiving
Help from a woman EMT
Or a woman patient being treated
By a male EMT will automatically
Respond to comforting physical
Gestures with flirtatious behavior.
Do not respond by flirting back.

ASK

Ask questions about an area
Or organ *before* you examine it.

Ask: What's your name?
    What's happening to you?
    Where were you going, or where
    Are you? Can you tell me the date
    (Day of the week, year)?
Document the patient's condition
Precisely—"disoriented to time."

Depending on the urgency of the situation,
Either ask yes-or-no questions
    ("Have you eaten today?" "Does it hurt
    When you move your arm?")
Or open-ended questions
    ("When does the pain come on?"
    "Tell me about your last meal").

How intense is the pain?
    Dull? Throbbing? Sharp?
    Crushing? Stabbing? Does
    The pain change in intensity
    Or remain constant? What
    Started it? How long ago?

RESPONSIVENESS

What can the patient feel?
Can he identify the stimulus?
How does he respond to pain?
With unconscious or sleeping patients,
Determine how easily
They can be aroused.
If they cannot be aroused
By verbal stimuli, can
They be aroused by a pain
Stimulus like a pinch?

If the patient does not respond
To voice, try pain.

Your patient is RESPONSIVE
If he seems to be unconscious but will:
- Open his eyes if you speak to him.
- Respond to a light touch on the hand.
- Try to avoid pain.

The answer you receive from the patient
When you ask, "Can you tell me where
You are hurt?" is the CHIEF COMPLAINT.
In many instances, this
Will be obvious, such as the patient
Who lies bleeding in the street
After being struck by an automobile.

Even in this circumstance, however,
It is useful to determine
What is bothering the patient most.

CHECK

Check the Facial Features.
Feel the Head and Neck.
Check the Clavicles and Arms.
Check the Chest. In injury
      Patients, feel for air
      Crackling beneath the skin.
Check the Abdominal Region.
      Sudden pokes will make
      The muscles tense.
Check the Pelvic Region
      For Tenderness. Damage here
      Can cause great pain,
      So be gentle.
Check the Back.
Check the Feet, Ankles, and Legs.

Describe pulse amplitude by using the following scale:
    4+ Bounding
    3+ Normal
    2+ Difficult to palpate
    1+ Weak and rapid, thready
    0 Absent

HELPFUL TIPS

Avoid traffic accidents
While going to the scene of an accident
Or to the hospital. Use a seat belt . . .
Park safely and carefully.

Check all equipment.
Keep the interior clean.
Are all your bandage wraps cleaned up?

If there is any question
About the patient's condition, assume
The worst and work from there.

If a patient requests
That you pray with him, do so.

LEGAL SITUATIONS

What Happens if a Patient
Files Suit? [How to document:]
        Draw a thin line
        Through an error.
        Never erase an error.

Another legal situation
Is death. If a person is obviously
Dead (crushed, decapitated,
Rigor mortis setting in),
You may be required
To leave the body at the site.

ANSWER

If death is imminent either
On the scene or in the ambulance,
Be supportive and reassuring
To the patient, but do not lie.

If a patient asks, "I'm dying,
Aren't I?" respond
With something like, "You
Have some very serious injuries,
But I'm not giving up on you."

AND BEAR IN MIND

The heart is a hollow, muscular
Organ the size of the fist.

Once the patient remains
In clinical death for a certain time
(Typically four to six minutes),
Brain cells begin to die.

Along the edges of the eyelids
Are openings of many small oil glands
Which help prevent the tears
From evaporating too rapidly.

A Letter to Theo

—V. van Gogh, letters, 1873–1890, edited by
I. Stone, translated by Johanna van Gogh

Oh, lad, I should like to have you here
To show you my lodgings. I have, for instance, real
Kitchen chairs, and a real strong kitchen table.

I am going to draw it, and work at it
Until I have fixed it on paper.

What is drawing? How does one learn it?
To better my life—don't you think I eagerly desire it?
Cannot I serve some purpose and be of any good?
Do you think we too shall be at the evening of our life?

There is a yellow sky over everything.
I am seeking for blue all the time.
I am thinking of planting two oleanders in tubs.
Perhaps I shall begin to look about for greens.

Why should not the shining dots of the sky
Be as accessible as the black dots on the map of France?

When shall I get back to that other world?
My God, where is my child? Is living alone
Worthwhile? And then I said to myself, You
Are not becoming melancholy again, are you?

So, lad, do come and paint with me
On the heath, in the potato field; come
And walk with me behind the plough and the shepherd.

I think so often of that walk on the Ryswyk road,
Where we drank milk after the rain, at the mill.

Language for Everyone

—Leonard Bloomfield, *Language*, 1933

(Boyibus kissibus priti girlorum, girlibus likibus, wanti somorum.)

PART ONE   JOHN RAN AWAY

Suppose we hear a speaker say
  John ran,
And a little later hear him or another speaker say
  John fell.
We recognize at once that these two forms,
John ran and *John fell,* are in part phonetically alike . . .
In fact, if we are lucky,
We may hear someone utter the form *John!*
All by itself, without any accompaniment.

John! John?
John?! ('It isn't John, I hope!')

John, he ran away.
Who was watching the door?

Who? With whom? Who ran away?
With whom was he talking?

PART TWO   THE LONE JILL

The lone Jill is in much
The same position as the speechless animal.
Bow-wow, whip-poor-will, gnaf-gnaf.

41

Money gave out . . .
Horses gave out.
That's all . . . One hardly knows what to say.

I am thinking of him. Charge
The man with larceny. Baby
Is hungry. Poor baby. I'm hungry
(Angry, frightened, sorry, glad;
My head aches, and so on).

"You haven't given me money to buy coal."
Sniff, sniffle, snuff, sizzle, wheeze.

I was just wishing I had an apple.

PART THREE   THE STUDY OF SPEECH

Since lips, tongue, and uvula are elastic,
They can be placed so that the breath
Sets them into vibration:

Choo-choo, bye-bye, goody-goody
Zigzag, flimflam, pell-mell.
Here are some apples; take one.

PART FOUR   HOW IT ALL ENDED

The man, who was carrying a bag,
Came up to our door.

John! John? John?! Shut the door.
King John, John Brown . . . Mount Everest.

Whatever he says, I don't believe him:

42

Ish gabibble, I love you.
An inanimate object is a roadster.
Man wants but little
Here below.
          Is zat so?

Baby is hungry. Give Baby the orange.
Give us bread and flesh. Poor baby.
 I don't seem to understand all you say.

          You angel. Here are some apples; take one.
          Heute spielen wir Ball. Ouch, damn it!
          It's high time we—it's high time we—

Is zat so? Please, "oxcuse" me.
Go without me. Go.
It is regrettable. Oh well, I guess
It won't matter. Choo-choo, bye-bye.

Wave your hand to Daddy.

ENVOY

What happened remains a secret.

Choo-choo, bye-bye, oxcuse me,
It's ten o'clock. I have to go.
One set of sounds is as unreasonable as any other.

Choo-choo, bye-bye, goody-goody,
Goodness gracious! dear me! Lickspittle,
Dreadnaught, snub-nosed, red-bearded,
Chortle, kodak, and *blurb.*

The Old Masters

—Robert Henri, *The Art Spirit* (compiled by his
student, Margery A. Ryerson), 1923

The old masters
Were not so nervous as we are.

VELASQUEZ: He must have felt
And willed all that he did.

COROT: The quality of mind
That makes you paint as you do is what counts.

MANET: Notice the meaning of every change.
HOGARTH: The head of a fish girl.

Here is a sketch by Leonardo da Vinci.
I enter this sketch

And I see him at work and in trouble
And I meet him there.

Otherwise It Would Be Too Confusing

—Elizabeth A. Ryan, *How to Make Grammar*
Fun—and Easy!, 1992

(The perception of a reasonably stable environment helps in
the assessment of a given situation. Otherwise it would be
too confusing to live for more than a few moments.)
—R. A. Padgham

Who or *what* receives the action? The *Frisbee.*
Whew, I thought I had lost it.

This is the place for me!
The *red* truck . . . the *starry* night . . .

I ran quickly through the *streets* and *byways.*
As I came through the door,
I said, "I *have come* home."

A *bunch/* of grapes/ *tastes* good after lunch.

That was a *good* song, and you sang it *well.*
That was a *bad* song, and you sang it *badly.*
Don't you feel *well*?
I am *sure.* I am *surely* in love.

Rita is a *friendly* person.
Cyanide is a *deadly* poison.
Right: *I* went to the store.
Wrong: *Me* went to the store.

Let go of that doorknob.
And remember: the Fourth of July.

A Visit to the Mayo Clinic

—Walter C. Alvarez, M.D. (Professor and
Consultant, the Mayo Clinic), *Nervousness,
Indigestion, and Pain*, 1943

ENTER THE PATIENTS

We physicians see nowadays: mildly insane
Persons; largely eviscerated persons; mercurial
Persons—tense, eccentric, constitutionally inadequate
And ne'er-do-well:
                              A nervous, tired little seamstress;
A sensitive, somewhat neurotic, middle-aged professor;
An attractive but frail and hypersensitive little violinist.
A scrawny woman, whose tissues were evidently made
Of poor materials. (Perhaps the hand of the Potter
Slipped a bit.) A frail, nervous little minister:

He blushed inside his bowel when embarrassed!
An apathetic man still wearing his galoshes;
A stupid hypochondriac with small earning power.

THEIR COMPLAINTS

Their excitement causes them to fill with gas;
They break into a sweat, the brain tightens.
Some persons feel a snake crawling 'round the abdomen.
Waves of gooseflesh; waves running up the esophagus;
A puzzling pain in the flank, a catch in the breath.

A swishing stomach: I told her that it was not
A disease but only an accomplishment without social value.

Is it real pain? Usually it is only an ache.
A burning, or a quivering, or a picking, pricking, pulling,
Pumping, crawling, boiling, gurgling, thumping,
Throbbing, gassy or itching sensation, or
A constant ache, strongly suggests neurosis.

A cold sweat, lumbago, cricks, wry neck.
Vertigo and feelings of uncertainty. Sometimes there
Are curious musical or squeaky or rubbing noises.

THE INTERVIEW

I like to find out how bad it is. Was there tragedy?
I like to know if the pain doubled the man up.
Did it ever cause him to get on his hands and knees?
I ask about sweating, palpitation, tingling in the legs.
Does he bloat? Does he at times feel unreal?

Has he succeeded in business? If not, why?

Is he unable to stick to any one thing?
Would he like to be a vagabond without responsibilities?

He cannot "take it." His tale of woe, which he thinks
Is so puzzling and rare, is an old story to me.

If the patient is a woman, is she sleeping with one eye open?
Ticklishness of the abdomen is interesting in women.

Was there any weakness of muscles? Does the limb get cold?
Did the patient suffer any heartbreaking psychic shock?

Is it burning, tearing, pressing, squeezing, or binding?
Is it due to too great tenseness, working late at night,
Worrying and thinking troublous thoughts, crying children?
Was there a tantrum? A picnic or cheap restaurant?

PERSONAL COMMENTS BY THE PHYSICIAN

Many a woman must know in her heart that she
Has messed up her life. If only these people would say
Less about quivering feelings in the abdomen.

ASSORTED DIAGNOSES

A diagnosis of psychoneurosis plus scatterbrainedness.
Years of foolish living with poor mental hygiene.
Pain due to feelings of rebellion.
Worry and fretting and trying to analyze Life.

She is just at the end of her rope nervously.
Often these women shop too long and too carefully.

He is too stupid, opinionated, ever to understand.

Debauchery due to loss of moral sense.
They were half crazy, undisciplined persons to begin with.

THE TREATMENT OF NERVOUS, PSYCHOPATHIC, POORLY ADJUSTED, MUCH TROUBLED OR OVERWORKED AND TIRED PERSONS

The cure for all this is more thinking. The thing to do
Is jump in and work. There is nothing like work for steadying.
The prognosis in these cases is poor. All treatment
Is likely to be futile. These persons are incurable.

These persons need to learn how to use their brains
More hygienically. Occasionally a blackberry cordial.

We Already Know You Like Baseball

—John Dewan, Don Zminda, and STATS, Inc., *The Stats Baseball Scoreboard*, 1990

(Hi, and welcome to our new book. We already know you like baseball.)

The higher the temperature,
The hotter the bats.
In '88, long flies
Stayed in the park more often.

Your eyes may well up with tears
Watching all the perfectly-laid bunts.

The White Sox brass wince.

Who can Pop in the Clutch?
Who Leads the League in Looking?
Can we learn anything from this?
Do Hitters Spend Most of their Time
Just Standing Around?

Do Sacrifices Sacrifice Too Much?
Will the Dome Lift the Jays to the Skies?

The Muse and the Poet

—Francis Buckland, *Buckland's Curiosities of Natural History,* 1858, 1860, 1865

STUFFED MERMAID

In an old curiosity-shop, in the west arcade
Of Hungerford Market (where they sell poultry),
I found my lady, looking as pretty as ever,

Under her glass case. Her head is too
Bullet-shaped, her eyes decidedly glass
Doll's eyes, her teeth a small bit of bone

Cut into notches, which detract from her interesting look;
But to make up for this, her hair is longer,
And her chest, etc, exceedingly well developed.

She is fastened upright by means of the curved
Portion of her tail, and smiles gracefully
Through her dusty glass house.

PET APE

I had at one time a very large fine ape.
Not wishing to lose sight of him altogether,
I made his skin into a mat for the table.

NIGHTINGALE

I no longer disbelieve the story of a man
Being specially retained by the proprietors of Vauxhall
To sit in a bush and sing like a nightingale. "Hear 'em,

Sir, why you're sure to hear 'em. We keeps
A nightingale." "Water-wabble-wabble—swatee."

ENVOY

But why remain here in the shallow water, my pretties?
Thousands and hundreds of thousands of your babies I have reared.

The Graduate Student: Aspects of the Tongue

—Robert Froriep, *Aspects of the Tongue,*
Bonn, 1828, translated by C. Garton and
J. D. Gerencser

I myself have drawn
With the utmost care and accuracy,
And have painted in color, all the pictures
Of tongues which I here submit.

A *pallid tongue:*
    Often appears in hypochondria.
A *red tongue:*
    A bad outlook.
A *very red tongue:*
    The illness is of a bad kind.

The *very red/scarlet tongue,*
A *very red/dark tongue:*
    The color of smoke-cured beef.
A *black/purple tongue,*
The *blue tongue,*
A *yellow tongue,*
A *light white coating:*
    Such a tongue would give very little ground for suspicion.
The *lardlike coating:*
    Very often stupor follows.
The *yellowish or green coating:*
    I dare not hazard an opinion.

An ashen coating,
A dark coating,
A black coating:
>   Occurs with some frequency. I am at pains
>   To recall to mind that external irritation
>   And frequent respiration of dry air
>   Very easily dries out the mucous
>   Which normally makes the mouth glisten
>   And makes it black.
>
>   This it was possible for me to observe
>   Especially on hiking expeditions
>   Of which I have made quite a lot.

A Natural History of Getting Through the Year

—William Alphonso Murrill, *The Natural History of*
Staunton, Virginia, 1919

NOVEMBER 1, 1895

The mountains are on fire
And everything is dry; insects gone.
My private work this year will be:
Biology, Bible, Art, Geology, Body,
Literature. This term will be devoted
To Art, Zoology, Bibles, Epics, Dramas,
Etc. I find the Entomostraca interesting.

JANUARY 24, 1896

I spent most of the day
Mounting butterflies from India.
This finishes all the flies for this year
Until more are caught.
Poisoned plants at night.
Very warm. The brightest,
Warmest January I remember.

PLAN OF NATURE STUDY FOR APRIL

Birds and flowers will keep one busy.
Make collections of both, and observe
The battles and songs of birds. Watch

For the eggs of Phoebe about the middle
Of the month. Study the circulation
Of the blood in a frog's foot.
Take up mental hygiene;
Because it is much needed now.

A View of Certain Wonderful Effects

—S. K. Heninger, Jr., *A Handbook of Renaissance Meteorology*, 1960 (spellings modernized)

THUNDER

It breaks through cloud. Thunder with his moving stirs
The brain, and fears the wit, and distroubles & stirs
And corrupts wine in tuns. And if it come
In breeding time of fowls, it grieves their eggs.

THUNDER AND LIGHTNING

The stars fall out of the firmament, and by the fall,
Both thunder and lightning are caused: for the lightning
Is nothing else but the shining of the star that falls,
Which falling into a watery cloud, and being
Quenched in it, causes great thunder.
(Even as hot iron makes a noise
If it be cast into cold water.)

LIGHTNING

This burns a man inward, and consumes the body
To ashes, without harming the garments; it stays
The youngling in the womb, without harm to the mother;
It consumes money, the purses remaining whole;
It harms the hand the glove not perished.

Getting Started

—David W. McKay and Bruce G. Smith, *Space Science Projects for Young Scientists*, 1986

Try dropping from different heights.
What do you observe? WHICH WAY IS DOWN?
Be careful selecting a place to perform this project.

Wear gloves and a plastic apron. Repeat the trial.
Wear earplugs. WEAR A FACE SHIELD AT ALL TIMES.
BE CAREFUL. THESE EXPERIMENTS ARE ADVANCED.

Try dropping from different heights. Imagine
How limited your knowledge of the world would be
If this were the only way you could gather information.

For example, what is on the other side
Of those trees? Try dropping from different heights.
If gravity were absent, what do you think would happen?

Now, drop the leaking can. Now,
Puncture the beach ball. Cut the garden hose.
Start the stopwatch. Grind up some cotton balls.

Try dropping from different heights. KEEP
YOUR FIRE EXTINGUISHER HANDY! Look closely.
Know where you can get help fast. Now try it.

From a Letter Home

—Holbrook Jackson, ed., *Bookman's Holiday*, 1946

The scarlet beans are up in crowds.
It has rained sweetly for two hours and a half;
The air is very mild. The heckberry
Blossoms are dropping off fast, almost gone;
Snowballs coming forward; May roses blossoming.
I have nobody now left but you.

I think of innumerable things; steal out
Westward at sunset, take oar, and row
In the dark or moonlight. In the evening I scribble
A little; all this mixed with reading.
I have a piano, but seldom play.
Books are becoming everything to me.

I stroll. I find the glades empty. I look
At every tree. O my dear bairn,
If I had thee here, I feel as if
I should be quite happy for a while.
I propose you come up here to live.
We will buy together five or six

Hundred acres, and have a sheep farm.
We shall have pleasant breakfasts, dinners.
Here we would have our books. Shall we not?
But this is too late. The fire is at
Its last click. Would this May weather last.
But June comes; the rabid dogs get muzzles.

Learning to Fear Watercolor

—Nicholson's Peerless Water Colors, instructions,
1991

PEERLESS WATER COLORS . . . The ONLY
Water Colors on FILM LEAFLETS.

Lay them on quickly. Begin.
They flow; they form shades and tints.

FLESH TINT: Be very careful
With this color. The tendency is
To get the wash too strong.

LIGHT GREEN: The tendency is
To get all greens too dark.

SKY BLUE: The tendency is
To color the sky too deeply. It must
Be well diluted and put on with great care.

SEPIA BROWN: Roadway, limbs
Of trees . . . a very serviceable color.
Much patience will be required.

DEEP BLUE: Very strong,
So use only small clippings.

Go at the work boldly. Cultivate
A free wrist movement. WE THANK YOU
For your interest in Peerless Colors
And hope you have enjoyed using them.

Always color your sky first—
Most fascinating, and so simple.

Index of First Lines

Join me in celebrating
Just there, in the corner of the whin-field
Like dolmens round my childhood, the old people.

My window shook all night in Camden town;
My world has been laid low, and the wind blows,
Now that the men have gone off to the choleric wars.

O country people,
O country people, you of the hill farms,
Our youth was gay but rough:
Passing through,
Pulling up flax.

Quick, woman, in your net,
Remember summer when God turned on the heat.

Someone else cut off my head.
Something is pushing against my blood.
So you are married, girl. It makes me sad.

The barman vaulted the counter.
The black fox loped out of the hills.

The rain comes flapping through the yard,
The spaceship drifting up,
The thing not done,
The tide gone out for good.

Was it a vision or a waking dream?
Was it wind off the dumps?
We approached the shore. Once more
We broke out of our dream into a clearing.
We left the western island to live among strangers.
What haunts me is a farmhouse among trees.

I Think Continually of Those Who Went Truly Ape

—Vitus B. Dröscher, *The Mysterious Senses of Animals,* translated by E. Huggard, 1965

During the hours of darkness all baboons
Suffer from a deep-rooted, primitive anxiety
Which continually startles them into wakefulness.

A deep, soft "O-O-O."
An appealing "la-la-la" cry.

A soft murmur among the crows, probably
Their love-talk. "Zick, zick, zick."

"Attention, please. I have just
Discovered a field of flowers.
It is buckwheat."

"Here I stand. Around me is my kingdom."
The male golden plover goes completely haywire.

"Ga, ga, ga, ga, ga, ga"
Means: "We feel comfortable here."
Five syllables means "The meadow grass is poor."

"Yup, yup, yup." "Kyah." "Kyoo."
A new day is dawning on the plain of Amboseli.

Building a Tree House

—D. C. Beard, *Shelters, Shacks and Shanties*, 1914

DWELLERS IN OUR CITIES

Dwellers in our cities do not seem to realize that there
Is any other life possible for them
Than a continuous nightmare existence amid monstrous
Buildings. Boys will do well to remember this.

AN OVERVIEW

Tree houses are used as health resorts. Recently
There was a gentleman of Plainfield living in a tree house
Because he found the pure air among the leaves beneficial.

The boys at Lynn, Mass., built a very substantial house
In the trees. Some New York City boys built a house
In the trees at One Hundred and Sixty-ninth Street, but here
The police interfered. There is now, or was recently,
An interesting tree house on Flatbush Avenue, Brooklyn.
Boys have proven they are perfectly competent.

APOLOGY AND INSTRUCTIONS

If the writer forgets himself once in a while and uses
Words not familiar to his boy readers, he hopes
They will forgive him.
                           In order to build a house
One must make one's plans *to fit the tree.*
This will be no bungling, unsightly piece of work.

Your tree-top house will stand the summer blows
And winter storms.
                              "Waney" is a good word, almost
As good as "sensiation." Don't select
A "waney" log. It is sometimes necessary in a two-tree
House to allow for the movement of the tree trunks.

The real old-fashioned axe is exceedingly useful.
I even have one now in my closet here
In the city of New York, but I keep it for sentiment's sake.

FURTHER NOTES

General Grant was not afraid of work.
Personally I do not like deception of any sort.
If you do not sleep well, you must blame the cook.

By the way, boys, the Indian with the load on his back
Is my old friend Bow-Arrow. I forgot to say
That the mountain goose is not a bird but a tree.

A COMICAL QUESTION FOR BOYS

Which would you rather do or go fishing?

ENVOY

The small boys who started at the beginning of this book
Are older and more experienced now. The reader
Must have, no doubt, noticed that problems become
More and more difficult as we approach the end.

Attempt to Move

—Max Picard, *The World of Silence*, 1948,
translated by Stanley Godman, 1952

Sometimes on a summer's day the village is sunk
In silence, as if sunk under the earth.

Sometimes there is a seat by the side of the road, with a cat
Resting on it. Each day appears unnoticed.

Sometimes the wall of a house stands in the light.
The spirit does not feel itself forsaken.

Sometimes in the city a man suddenly collapses
And dies in the midst of the noise of the highway.

Sometimes when the sea outside is calm,
Sometimes the frozen ships attempt to move.

How to Make a Visit to The Netherlands

—Hendrik Willem Van Loon, *An Indiscreet Itinerary,* 1933

"But this is absurd! We are sailing right over
The roofs of the houses!" But it is not absurd.

You need not feel you have separated yourself
From the rest of the world and will never see
Your loved ones again. People live constantly
Beneath the sombre skies of these water-soaked regions.
You will find the people to be cordial and well-
Disposed towards strangers (except on Thursday).

Near Amsterdam, watch the water of the canals.
That light is found only hovering over
This mud, floating on an ocean of water.
Quiet is the watchword of those canals.

Such experiences as these are worth
All the trouble of leaving home
And mother and the old familiar scenes.

"Ah, what is he talking about, anyway?"
You had better consult your little guide book.

Make friends with the porter. I would advise
You to spend one day walking around.
When you have had your fried sole, walk back
To town and once more sit ye down.

And now cometh the question, Whither
Are we bound? Rotterdam, The Hague.

You will be sure that your chauffeur is going
To pitch you into a canal. Don't be scared,
They never do, but it is just one
Of their little jokes, like that cracking of the neck,
So dear to the hearts of otherwise harmless osteopaths.

Just now what we need so terribly badly
Is a new point of view. At least, I hope so.

The Writing Life

—Samuel A. Thorn and Carl D. Duncan, *Let's Discover More*, 1957

Drop some oil on a piece of white notebook paper.

Rub your pencil very hard against a piece of tissue paper.
Put the tissue paper against the wall.

Bring in an eggbeater.

    Keep a record of the clouds you see.
    Put water and gravel into a dishpan.

    Break apart stones to see if they contain fossils.
    Break apart a lump of coal.
    Find the Milky Way.

    Click two marbles together softly.
    Sit facing a wall.

Do you see the speck of light
In the center of the circular paths?
Is the instrument beaten or shaken or blown into?
Notice that when you push down, the book moves up.
Have you also gained a change of direction?

Cut finger holes in a large piece of cardboard.
Hold the cardboard over your head while you run.

Name some other modern ways of telling stories.

Pastoral

—Max Picard, *The World of Silence*, 1948,
translated by Stanley Godman, 1952

Sometimes when a peasant moves with the plough and the
     oxen
Over the broad surface of the field,
It is as if the vault of the sky might take

Up into itself the peasant, the plough, and the oxen.
It is as though time had been sown into silence.
The eye of the gods falls on the figures and they

Increase. A bird flies slowly into the sky.
Its movements are trails that keep the silence enclosed.
Grain and stars shine through the mist and haze.

Animals lead silence through the world of man.
The cattle: the broad surface of their backs . . .
It is as if they were carrying silence.

Two cows in a field moving with a man beside them:
It is as if the man were pouring down silence
From the backs of the animals on to the fields.

The Naturalist at Large on the Delaware River

—Charles C. Abbott, M.D., *Waste-land Wanderings,* 1887

CONFESSIONS

I once witnessed a riot in wrendom.
I have insisted that the cardinal-redbird
Is not a mocker. I take it all back.

I am free to confess that woodpeckers
Have failed to interest me.
I know of two fine bowlders in the meadows,

But I use them only for stepping-stones—
Never as texts. My last public talk
About them was disastrous.

I saw a purple grackle's nest.
I resolved to climb the tree.
The birds looked on approvingly.

It now remained for me to descend.
Through some strange miscalculation
I failed to secure a footing, and fell.

The scars on my back made an excellent
Map of the Micronesian archipelago.
It most vividly recalled

The apparently instant appearance
Of every woman in the village
When my horse ran away and landed me
In the duck-pond on the common.

ANOTHER CONFESSION

In numerous little sink-holes,
I find the skeletons of small fishes.
I pick them from the mud.

The imprint of their shriveled
Forms is left—fossil
Impressions for the naturalist

Of ten thousand years to come.
This is possible, of course, so
I wrote on the smooth surface

From which I lifted a minnow,
Fundulus multifasciatus.
Will it not startle the paleontologist

Of the indefinite future to chisel
From rock an already labelled fossil?
I trust that he will not go mad.

LATE WANDERINGS

Now that nesting is over, many
Find next to nothing to sing about.

When a blast from the north blows
The brown rushes, above the roar

Can be heard a tone of sadness,
A cry, "We weep! we weep!"

"Keep up, keep up, keep!"
"Chesapeake, O Chesapeake!"

Was there not yet something
That I could watch even
By the gloaming's uncertain and waning light?

Deathbeds

—Edward S. Le Comte, ed., *Dictionary of Last Words*, 1955

(The poet essentially can't be concerned with the act of dying.)
—Henry James, preface to *The Wings of the Dove*

This is too tight; loosen it a little. I pray
You give me some sack! Bring me last year's apple,
If you can, or any new melon. A dozen cold oysters.
My children! My papers! My book, my unfinished book!

From my present sensations, I should say I was dying
—And I am glad of it. The world is bobbing around.

Do you know the Lord's Prayer? Cover me.
Shut the door. Can't see you any more.
I must go home. I am very forlorn at the present
Moment, and wish I was at Malvern.

Am I still alive? Do I drag my anchors?

So here it is at last, the distinguished thing!
Is this dying? Is this all? Is this
All that I feared, when I prayed against a hard death?
O! I can bear this! I can bear it!
Now I have finished with all earthly business
—High time, too. Yes, yes,
My dear child, now comes death.
Is it come already? Here, here is my end.
Wait a moment. Do you not hear the voices?
And the children's are the loudest! The chariots

And horses! I do not know how this happened.
I can account for it in no way.

Watty! What is this? It is death.
They have deceived me. It has all been very interesting.
I should like to have a good spin down Regent Street.
Four o'clock? How strange! So that is Time!

Sing to me, if you have the heart. Draw
The curtain. Turn me over. Perhaps I may
Sleep a little. Cover me up warm,
Keep my utterance clear . . . I'm doing well.

Ah, Catherine, how beautiful you look.
Yes, love, yes. Oh! dear. Good-bye,
Harry. Good-night, Lushington. I wish
Johnny would come. Will you please turn
This way? I like to look at your face.

Already my foot is in the stirrup. Lift
Me up, lift me right up! Now farewell.
We are over the hill; we shall go better now.

I am coming, Katie! John, it will not
Be long. Supremely happy! Excellent!
My dearest, dearest Liz. We are all going;
We are all going; we are all going.

This is it, chaps. Take me home.
I believe, my son, I am going. That's it.
Good-bye—drive on. Cut her loose, Doc.

I'm going, I'm going. At a gallop!
Clear the way. Good-bye, God bless you!
Good-bye, everybody. A general good-night.